# Advance Praise

"Bill Jones opens *Still Life in a Hurricane* with 'In the Near-Lost Memory Mine,' and his poems are gems found in that mine. With humor and poignancy, he writes about family elders and their emotional bequests to him. 'In a Prayer to St. Anthony,' he evokes his grandmother and a prayer she taught him: 'Saint Anthony, please help me find what I have lost.' In this delightful collection, Jones does indeed find what he has lost, and readers will be moved to do the same in their own lives."

> —Anne Higgins, Poet, Author of 9 books of poetry, most recently, *Not Only/But Also*

"Bill Jones's sense of purpose in *Still Life in a Hurricane* is evident in his dedication: 'Again, for my family.' It can be said that Jones has also made this collection *of* his family, of deep relationship: back to his forebears, over his long marriage, forward to the blessing of grandchildren, extending to the community of poets. The 'still life' formed of these narratives is richly detailed, memories and dreams brought forward—always with warmth, sometimes with humor—'into the light/ and air' of the page."

> —Madeleine Mysko, Author of the novels *Bringing Vincent Home* and *Stone Harbor Bound* and the poetry collection *Crucial Blue*

"Dylan—the poet disguised as a song and dance man—scraped and begged before the Queen Jane of his imagination for just a few moments of her time. Bill Jones did not have to conjure—approximately or precisely—the Jane without whom he would not be Bill. In *Still Life in a Hurricane*, she is here—stanza after stanza, from West Virginia and South America to the king-sized bed of his dreams. With Jane—lover and wife—Jones documents adventures domestic and worldly that could not have been taken without her. Or at least not ones this good."

> —Rafael Alvarez, Author, *Basilio Boullosa Stars in the Fountain of Highlandtown*

"If you don't already know Bill Jones, in reading *Still Life in a Hurricane*, you're about to. And very well. You'll know the roster of his childhood sins, the glory of his boyhood on Maryland shores, the whirlwind of his travels, the disorientation of his dreams and adventures. You'll learn of his love and meet his family. Jones's heart embraces a range of generations and hemispheres, engulfing dream worlds, rendering for us the results of vision, bravery, and generosity in this writing. *Still Life in a Hurricane* is a reckoning, a love letter, an act of courage, a gentle companion into the unknown. It is what we are always feeling, even under clearest skies. It is the song we realize we are dancing to, under a night sky where the wishing stars give way to their surrounding black."

—Barbara DeCesare, Poet, Author of *Jigsaw Eyesore* and *Silent Type*

"A writer's ultimate triumph is to enable the reader to not only see and understand the world from his perspective, but to enable readers to see their own world from a better perspective for having read his work. Bill Jones does this again and again in *Still Life in a Hurricane*. Jones transforms memory, humor, loss, and the everyday into extraordinary moments; through this powerful collection, he elevates the mundane and the profane into the holy. Jones beckons us to stop, perk our ears and train our vision, to see into the past and be present in what's right now, all around us, and revel in this glorious life by immersing ourselves in it. *Still Life in a Hurricane* beckons the reader to acknowledge the beauty of the storm, the eye, the aftermath, and the recovery. It reminds us that the best part of being human is being."

—Matt Hohner, Poet, Author of *States and Thresholds and Other Poems*

# Still Life in a Hurricane

# Still Life in a Hurricane

## Bill Jones

Apprentice
House Press
*Loyola University Maryland*

First Edition

Paperback ISBN: 978-1-62720-206-0
Ebook ISBN: 978-1-62720-207-7

Printed in the United States of America

Designed by Cara Hullings
Edited and promoted by Dani Williams
Cover photo: Bill Jones
Author photo: Jane C. Jones

Published by Apprentice House Press

Apprentice
House Press
*Loyola University Maryland*

Apprentice House Press
Loyola University Maryland
4501 N. Charles Street
Baltimore, MD 21210
410.617.5265 • 410.617.2198 (fax)
www.ApprenticeHouse.com
info@ApprenticeHouse.com

# Contents

## I

In the Near-Lost Memory Mine ............................................................... 3

First Confession, Age 7 ......................................................................... 4

Listening, 8 Years Old ............................................................................ 6

Playing Right ............................................................................................ 7

Why I Can't Recite This Poem from Memory ..................................... 8

Why I'm Not in the Basketball Hall of Fame ..................................... 9

## II

Why William Wordsworth Never Lived in Baltimore ....................... 13

The Benefit ............................................................................................ 14

Car Crash, Christmas Eve .................................................................... 15

Don't Consider This .............................................................................. 16

Manta Ray .............................................................................................. 18

Thought, With the Children Gone ....................................................... 19

In the Heat at Crazy Ray's ................................................................... 20

Thought, Skydiving .............................................................................. 22

For the Record ....................................................................................... 24

For Jane, After Fifty Years ................................................................... 25

## III

A Prayer to Saint Anthony ................................................................... 29

My Laws, Grandmother Jones ............................................................. 30

My Grandfather Ulpiano ...................................................................... 32

My Last Visit with My Grandfather Jones .......................................... 33

My Mother Spoke of Guayaquil .......................................................... 35

Pietà ....................................................................................................... 36

How I Picture My Father ...................................................................... 37

## IV

First Night at The Irotama ................................................................... 41

In Santa Marta, Gambling ................................................................... 43

Spring Rafting on the New ................................................................... 45

Still Life in a Hurricane ............................................................... 46

The Woman with Needs ............................................................... 48

Outside the Visitor Center  .......................................................... 50

Found Poem: Signs on the Pacific Coast Scenic Byway.................. 51

## V

Dream Poem: The Dancing Trees................................................... 55

Dream Poem: The Jones Falls........................................................ 56

Dream Poem: Going Off the Meds................................................ 57

Dream Poem: Picture Day............................................................. 58

Dream Poem: Waves on the Thirtieth Floor .................................. 60

## VI

Advice and Guarantee Wastecan ................................................... 65

He Sensed He Was in Trouble ....................................................... 66

Dear Mail Lady  ........................................................................... 67

The Perfect American Poem .......................................................... 68

The Man Who Couldn't Stop Revising........................................... 69

## VII

Age 65, With Both Parents Gone................................................... 73

How I Hope It Will Be.................................................................. 74

A Promise to My Grandchildren ................................................... 75

Reading the Paper, 66 .................................................................. 76

Like Thomas, Reading Signs......................................................... 77

Two Rosaries................................................................................ 78

Something Almost Spiritual........................................................... 79

Acknowledgments........................................................................ 81

About the Author......................................................................... 85

*Again, for my family*

# I

*"Things that I grew up with stay with me."*

Tim Burton

# In the Near-Lost Memory Mine

It's dark down here,
and my headlamp's old
and flickering, often going out.
Stumbling through rubble
in the pitch-black,
I'm crawling under caved-in timbers,
my face shrouded
in grit and cobwebs.

As bats screech, drop,
and wing away,
I'm struggling
through openings
just large enough
for my shoulders.
I'm ready
to get out of here.

But then I hear
the voices again,
sometimes only audible
as whispers, begging
to be brought back
to the surface
into the light
and air.

# First Confession, Age 7

*(St. John the Evangelist Roman Catholic Church, Frederick, MD, 1958)*

*Bless me, Father, for I have sinned;*
*this is my first confession.*

I'd kept a tally for weeks
so I was ready when called
out of the pew
where I had been waiting.

*I was mean to my brother and sister—*
*11 times.*

I'd been sitting with all the other boys in uniform,
blue slacks, white starched shirts,
blue clip-on ties with a little white cross
circled by St. John's School on a patch.

*I have disobeyed my mother and father—*
*22 times.*

I'd watched the girls go into the confessional
and come out looking serious
for their trip to the altar rail to kneel
and do their penance,

*I have had impure thoughts—*
*33 times.*

and I'd stood in line with my fellow male sinners,
straining to hear what they were saying inside that box,
wondering if there were any Godforsaken
murderers among us,

*I have taken the Lord's name in vain—*
*44 times.*


and back in our seats, I wouldn't tell, no matter how often
Chip Clendaniel whispered, "What did you get?"
that all I'd been sentenced to for my mountains of sin
was ten Hail Marys and five Our Fathers.

*I have told lies*
*on occasion.*


After all, the surly Sisters had pronounced
that revealing our penance
would be yet another
serious offense.


*For these and all my sins,*
*I am most heartily sorry.*

# Listening, 8 Years Old

*(Dividing Creek, MD, 1959)*

One hour before dawn, Cousin Paul and Tom
sleep-talk in their sandy beds.

An alarm sounds, a Norelco buzzes,
Uncle Harold rustles into suit and tie.

In the dark kitchen, a light flashes,
a handle clunks on the Frigidaire.

My grandmother whispers goodbye to Harold,
the screen door creaks open and shut.

The Belair, white and aqua, cranks,
comes to life, takes off for Baltimore.

Awake in his bedroom, my grandfather coughs,
clearing years of Camels.

Pots clink softly, silver is sorted—
the scent of Maxwell House fills the air.

Down by the pier, gulls wheel above the seaweed
as peeler crabs flicker backfins across the surface.

Next door at Lamberts', a bobwhite,
perched on the pump handle, calls his name.

On the porch, in a cage, muffled by green silk night,
Petey, the canary, waits to sing.

# Playing Right

Summer mornings meant fateful minutes
of standing around home plate
as two captains picked their teams.
I was always last and usually a throw-in
when the number of kids wasn't even.


*Play right*, my unlucky captain would growl,
banishing me to that place for chumps
who couldn't catch or throw
or do anything useful for a team of 6- to 12-year-olds
who played in the neighborhood.


At bat, I'd swing and miss
or hit a weak dribbler to the pitcher
as the other kids groaned and grumbled
back into the field,
our half-inning over.


Only once did I play
catch with my father,
who came home tired from a ten-hour day
and was nagged by my mother into going
outside with a ball.


With his old glove and a catcher's mitt,
he threw to me, a kid afraid
of anything harder than a toss,
a child who flinched and headed inside
when his pitches stung my hand.


Years later, with my youngest son,
I'd catch and throw for hours.
Coaching his team, I'd stand on third,
windmilling with joy,
sending happy children home.

# Why I Can't Recite This Poem from Memory

This history teacher,
who will go unnamed,
knew her facts and subject matter,
but she never understood what mattered most
to St. John's eighth-grade boys.

As punishment, she'd keep us after school
and make us memorize her
chosen poems, demanding that we study
for as long as it would take
to recite them perfectly.

Today I can't remember much
of any of those poems, just the first two lines
of "In Flanders Fields" and "Stopping by Woods...."
Sandburg, Dickinson, Shakespeare, Poe
have blown away like chalk dust.

Now I can recall prayers
and the first stanza of a song or two,
but I can't summon much more
than the opening lines of poems,
including my own.

Yes, this history teacher will stay
unnamed, lost,
I guess, in history.
I thank God she didn't punish us
by making us write.

# Why I'm Not in the Basketball Hall of Fame

With a minute to go against South Carroll High,
I was stripped of the ball and they scored.
With three seconds left,
I hit the winning jumper from the top of the key.
Coach Pansa ran onto the court and hugged and kissed me.


But that didn't translate
into much playing time
for a JV point guard, 5'7", 145,
who couldn't dribble
worth a damn.


When *The Hagerstown Herald* recorded
my other great moment–
fifteen points against St. Maria Goretti–
it reported my name
Jill Bones.

# II

*"Take care of all your memories...*
*For you cannot relive them."*


Bob Dylan

# Why William Wordsworth Never Lived in Baltimore

*(Charles Village, Baltimore, MD, 1973)*

It was cool up there,
and I could see the stars
and nearly see the harbor
after I'd climbed out the window,
up the fire escape,
and onto the baked tar roof.
And that October night
I might have stayed a while
if it hadn't been for the sudden
thunder of copter blades,
the spotlight on my face,
and the cop on a bullhorn yelling,
*You, on the roof, get down from there,*
*right now.*
Yeah, I might have stayed out
for an hour or two,
maybe even written a poem.

# The Benefit

*(Baltimore Museum of Art, 1979)*

It's a steaming August
night in Baltimore,
and the gates of the Museum of Art
are closed.

A jazz trio's playing
in the sculpture garden
where couples sip chablis
and sample food
served on silver platters
by waiters
in black and white.

Outside the fence,
four eight-year-old boys
in poor-kid clothes
abandon their bikes
and press their faces
against the wrought iron,
staring in.

*Hey mister, can we
have some of that?*
one boy calls.

Inside, pretending
not to hear or see,
nobody answers.
After all, this is
a benefit.

# Car Crash, Christmas Eve

*(Towson, MD, 1986)*

Up on its side,
wheels still spinning,
spinning,
his green Plymouth
balanced itself
on the hillside
heavy with oak.
He had shot
through the hospital's castle gate
and across four lanes of traffic
with two white Fords
in hot pursuit,
security men in a sweat.
With one last swerve,
he'd put her up on that hill
and then climbed out
in an aqua robe
and leather smoking slippers,
his head a gyroscope
veering out of kilter.
Four county cops cruised up,
flicked off their sirens
and cigarettes,
and then all closed in
around his form,
sweet antic death,
dancing in silk
and strobes of blue
as he chanted like a child
whose wires were crossed
that all was calm,
yes, all was bright,
on that night
so far from silent.

# Don't Consider This

*(Baltimore, MD, 1993)*

Don't consider this
metaphor.
Consider it truth.

Consider 103 degrees in August,
me sitting at a red light at Lake and Charles,
windows up, AC blasting full,
a summer storm ripping in
two minutes to the north–
wind, low rumble, flash.

Consider on my left,
some 50 feet above the earth,
a man suspended
by rope and harness
in an oak tree sheared of limbs
and ready to come down.

Consider the man's right hand.
From it dangles a chainsaw
while his left seems to be gesturing
not to me or his coworkers on the ground
but to some figure above
that only he can see.

Consider then his face,
a mask of stinging, burning bees.
As the rising winds play havoc
with the lines his friends
can't untangle,
his only cry is *Down!*

Consider fists of rain
thundering to the ground.
Consider again the bees.
Consider the light
finally turning green
and me driving like hell for home.

# Manta Ray

*(Ocean City, MD, 2002)*

Near midnight
around the fishing pier,
floodlights have turned
the ocean into coffee.
Out on the end, spectators
gather in silence as men and boys
cut squid, hook frozen shiners,
and cast them out.

When a church group passes
through the gates of the tackle shack,
an eight-year-old points
beyond the breakers, crying,
*It's a manta ray!*
but I don't believe until I see
that diamond shape gliding
beneath the surface.

Six feet across, it circles
at the edge of the light,
the white tips of its wings
sometimes breaking water.
The dock crew scrambles
to get a look, and one fool
forty-year-old tosses
a lure in its direction.

Twice more that night
the fish appears,
beyond where any hooks can reach,
a tan ghost
rising from the deep,
giving us a glimpse of God,
then diving into
darkness.

# Thought, With the Children Gone

*(7 a.m., Union River Bay, ME, August 12, 2012)*

It's quiet in the house,
our vacation nearly over,
the children gone,
Sara, Mike, and Nathan, in the dark,
Sean and Melissa just now,
an hour after dawn.

Their rooms in order,
beds stripped,
closets empty,
their cars rolled quietly
down the gravel road
through the birch and pines.

Jane's sleeping,
her face as composed
as an angel's,
untroubled by the loss I feel,
the sense that our times
like these are numbered.

Outside, in early light,
jays flicker through the trees.
Two does make their silent way
across the pebble beach.
As happens every morning,
the tide is heading out.

# In the Heat at Crazy Ray's

*(Baltimore, MD, 2013)*

"This heat brings out the madness," I tell the man sitting next to me in the dust and diesel fumes. He doesn't say a word.

This morning in July, the temperature is 101, and I've made my way through East Baltimore to the wasteland, Crazy Ray's, where they promise four hundred dollars for any vehicle you can drag onto the lot. I've brought in Lucky, our 15-year-old Corolla, whose lease on life has ended.

Beneath a halo of razor wire, I present myself to Ronald, a short, black man, maybe twenty-two, who runs the outside operation. In an air-conditioned bunker, the men with the money wait. With dreads, no sleeves, and a white towel over his head, Ronald keeps the line moving, standing behind a school-kid's desk, trying to stay cool.

"You got a title for that?" he asks, pointing at Lucky, and when I say I do, our deal's as good as done. "Pull it over there, take off the tags, and fill these out," he rattles off, handing me pliers, a screwdriver, a clipboard, two forms in triplicate, and a pen. When I'm finished, he sends me to the bench with the man who will not speak and gets right back to work.

A white couple from Hampden, covered in tattoos, negotiates with him, hoping for a miracle as they try to sell their wheels. "Next," Ronald demands.

A Korean minister steps up in a linen suit and tie. "Can you get me one of these?" he asks, holding out an engine part wrapped in a white handkerchief. Ronald points at the commandment—U Pick It, U Pull It—on a sign above his head. "Next."

"You always puttin' it to de little mon!" a Jamaican protests to Ronald as the two vehicles he's brought in rumble in the road. "You say four hundred but take off for ev'ry dis and dot!" Ronald looks him in the eyes and growls, "That one's got no muffler. The revolution's over. Next."

"Can you say excuse me?" a local guy thunders at a jet-black man who's brushed into him near the stacked, used anti-freeze. "These Africans, we need to teach them manners," he announces to the crowd. "First we try the easy way, then we try the hard."

"Excuse me! Excuse me!" The African takes up the challenge. "Please and thank you, American!" he shouts, his voice in the shape of a fist. Ronald restores order with a stare.

"Wait over there," he commands as he hands me a yellow receipt, and I head to the office door where five minutes later, a guy with a tie steps out of darkness and hands me cash.

Leaving the lot in the noontime haze, I wipe my forehead and watch a forklift pierce old Lucky, lift him fifteen feet in the air, and take him over the gravel ridge to his final resting place.

"This heat brings out the madness," I mutter to myself, praying that my ride comes soon. Lord knows, I can't get Lucky.

# Thought, Skydiving

*(October 22, 2017)*

I had dreamed of this moment for years,
the plunging from the plane
some two miles up,
the falling, falling, falling,
and then the catch and clunk
of the chute opening,

the gazing at the October landscape—
brown fields sheared of corn,
forests flaming orange, yellow, lime,
and in the distance, the Chesapeake
and the Susquehanna
shimmering silver.

What I hadn't dreamed of
was having to sit in
the doorway of the plane,
my legs wrapped beneath it,
waiting to go, and of the backflip
the instructor told me

we'd be doing as we launched.
When I heard about that flip,
I decided to shut my eyes
and keep them shut until I felt
that we were stable, free-falling
parallel to the ground.

Photos of those flipping moments
show the plane, the Earth and sky
in changing places,
my face serene and joyful,
and I was, anticipating light
and beauty soon to follow.

And at that moment,
I swear to you, I was thinking
of my final fall, and I believed
that then, too, facing fear
could be as simple
as closing my eyes.

# For the Record

*(2018)*

My grandson, Garrett, 4, plays "guys" with Legos and Star Wars stuff. He laughs at jokes and sight gags, loves absurdities in *Highlights*, reports to Nan the things that Granddad says. At 2, he hesitated to climb the ladder on a slide. Now he climbs a 40-foot wall, rappels down and starts up the wall again. His favorite phrase? *Watch this.*

My granddaughter, Molly, 2, scrambles out of her crib onto beds over the couch up the bookshelves through the toys. She turns out the lights in the dining room to sing "Happy Birthday" to an invisible cake, blows out the candles, turns on the lights, and starts it all again. When offered help, she refuses with her favorite phrase—*I do it.*

My grandson, Conor, 1 day old, sleeps as only infants can, at peace, his face aglow, his breathing quick and quiet. His eyelids quivering like a butterfly's wings, he dreams of a world beyond all words, a place we can only imagine.

# For Jane, After Fifty Years

*(March 28, 2018)*

Lying in bed tonight at midnight
with you asleep in my arms,
I drift back

to that first December in the cabin in the snow,
with pillows and blankets and the fireplace,
*Electric Ladyland* in the air,

and to that warm March afternoon in Gambrill,
both of us home from college, celebrating early spring
beneath blue skies and leafless oaks,

and to The Island Beachcomber in St. Thomas,
you beautiful, asleep, as I stepped out onto the shore
for my first sunrise over the Caribbean,

and to the room on the point at The Reefs in Bermuda,
and the cottage in Port Antonio where we woke
to the sound of peacocks and the sight of azure sea,

and to the coastal cliffs of Oregon and Maine,
the snow chutes on Rainier, Going to the Sun in Glacier,
the shells in Sanibel.

Lying in bed tonight with you at midnight,
I think of those places we've been together, finding ourselves
in love.

# III

*"Remembering is holy ground."*

Malcolm Boyd

# A Prayer to Saint Anthony

*(in memory of Anastasia Lyng Coronel, 1895-1986)*

Irish Catholic, my Grandmother Coronel
would sit in a rocker
each afternoon for an hour,
her worn prayer book in her hands,
a rosary of black glass beads
draped around her knuckles
as she sought solace
in Our Lady.

On her bureau stood
a crucifix from Ecuador,
where my mother had been born,
with Christ so grim and ghastly
that I couldn't draw my eyes away
from the broken skull nailed beneath His feet
or the crimson streaming from His knees,
battered as He staggered to Golgotha.

In a bureau drawer
lay my grandmother's relics,
cloths that had touched a saint's remains,
holy water blessed by the pope.
I remember walks to church–Immaculate Heart,
Saint William of York–and one bus trip
to the Shrine of Saint Jude,
the Patron Saint of Lost Causes.

Years later, with her parents,
my grandfather, and her four sisters gone,
she taught me the prayer to say
when something I really needed disappeared.
Armed with faith and ready
to be taken, my grandmother passed away at 91.
*Saint Anthony, please help me find*
*what I have lost.*

# My Laws, Grandmother Jones

*(in memory of Evelyn Messersmith Jones, 1900-1972)*

*My Laws*, my grandmother says,
not wanting to take His name in vain
or teach grandchildren bad habits.
I see her now in the kitchen doorway
at the shore, presiding over the table,
where on a good day, twelve of us
are gathered.

Or she's in the door of the porch,
clanging the bell for all of us
to come up from the water for lunch
before we head back out onto the pier
to sit, our feet dangling over the water,
as we wait for her to clang again,
our hour up so we can go back swimming.

And evenings, when supper's over, the dishes done,
on the porch in her rocker,
she's swapping tales with the adults,
with me hoping she'll find something funny
because I'm sure her deep, deep laugh,
will lift the roof and find its way
to heaven.

In her last years, she's doting on my grandfather,
fixing him warm milk each morning,
frying him the tripe he loves
or soft crabs we've netted in the early tides.
She's a lady with terrible hot flashes,
who mops her face with her apron ends.
She doesn't sweat, she *perspires*.

Then I begin to notice she's been crying,
exchanging sad glances with her only daughter, Dorothy.
Before her final surgery,
my grandmother calls family and friends,
inviting them to her funeral.
She seems certain that she won't survive,
and My Laws, she is right.

# My Grandfather Ulpiano

*(in memory of Ulpiano Coronel Zevallos, 1896-1968)*

When she said to me, *You're going to be just like him,*
my mother was probably thinking about her father
as that stormy man
who never seemed at home in the world.

But I prefer to think of him
as the man who, as a teenager,
came to this country from Ecuador
against his father's wishes,

who learned English
in a machine shop in Baltimore,
sharpened his vocabulary by reading Poe,
earned a degree at Maryland,

became the chief civil engineer
in the country of his birth,
and then, back in America, helped to design
the Chesapeake Bay Bridge.

And I think of the man
who took me alone as a 10-year-old
to Vellegia's and the 40,000 Fathoms
to introduce me to the pleasure of fine food,

who taught me to play chess
while he patiently puffed
on Cuban cigars or his pipes
of Cherry Blend tobacco,

or who, in my favorite Christmas Eve memory,
read St. John's version of the Nativity
from our family Bible
to the three of us, his grandchildren.

# My Last Visit with My Grandfather Jones

*(in memory of William Irving Jones, 1891-1976)*

He sat by the window
and spoke of the things he saw—
the hay fields and the horses,
in the distance, the Rappahannock,
where he had driven loads of lumber
down from his father's mill.

His eyes cleared as he talked,
his soft white hair trimmed neatly,
his small frame looking smaller
in the foolish gown he wore.
He spoke of the family, a reunion in Saluda—
Uncle Alvin with his glass left eye,
tobacco splattered on a closed car window,
hell raised with my father,
the kid who had washed that car;

Randolph-Macon,
Baltimore Business College—
chosen by two sisters, Ruby and Pearl,
who thought it best for a bright young boy
to get away from the farm,
to leave off field work and planing beams
for bookkeeping and accounting columns.

In a few minutes, my grandfather grew tired.
Lifting him beneath each shoulder,
we helped him stand up from his chair.
With one of us on each side of him,
he moved slowly to his bedside.
He paused, caught his breath,
then pushed himself up backwards
into his bed again.

Before we left the room,
I walked over to the window.
Far from the Rappahanock,
far from Saluda and Uncle Alvin,
the hay fields and the horses,
I sought an old man's vision
in the hospital parking lot.

# My Mother Spoke of Guayaquil

My mother spoke of Guayaquil,
Quito, Cuenca, Riobamba,

sites of mystery and myth from her life
in Ecuador. She told us tales

of her father going to work at dawn in a canoe
and returning at sunset on horseback,

of the local swimming pool boiling away
beneath a lava flow,

of her parents' gift of a puppy,
a Galápagos wild dog,

of playing basketball and singing
with Belgian nuns at school,

of sleeping under mosquito nets
to avoid malaria,

of bottle feeding an orphaned fawn
until it ate her mother's curtains,

and, of course, of living with her *abuelita*,
Deifilia, the grandmother she revered.

# Pietà

*(New York World's Fair, Flushing Meadow, NY, 1964)*

The room is blue, deep blue,
the color of the sky at nightfall.
Four hundred lights flicker like stars,
crowning the ceiling
and streaming down the walls.

The statue is softly lit, glowing white,
Mary, grieving, seated,
her Son's body in her arms.
Her face, bowing down,
shares her sorrow.

The room is silent, deeply silent,
as hundreds of visitors glide by
on moving walkways.
In the presence of such sacred art,
my own mother's face is radiant.

# How I Picture My Father

1925, at the farm in Saluda, with family elders who have dressed for the occasion. In a sailor suit, a box camera in his hand, he's the four-year-old in the front row sticking out his tongue.

1935, at All Saints School in Baltimore, in line with friends who will last a lifetime. His hair slicked and parted carefully, he's serious in his coat and tie, his eighth grade diploma in hand.

1945, in Hamborn, Germany, an Army Airborne medic in a wool winter uniform, standing by an ambulance before heading to Berlin.

1949, in Atlantic City, in a buggy with a fake dappled horse, posing with my mother, beaming, beneath the sign—"Just Married."

1958, St. Francis-like, extending his hand to mallards by the pier on Dividing Creek.

1962, in Frederick, in the bedroom doorway, pretending to play reveille to wake my brother and me.

1966, with tears on his face as he watches his Uncle Andrew's coffin leave All Saints.

1977, in *The Baltimore Sun*, reaching his hands in rubber gloves into a sealed glass box as he sets up an electron microscope for DNA research.

1986, retired, grinning, his green ball cap cocked at a jaunty angle as he sits astride a camel in Morocco.

1992, with bows and birthday ribbons draped around his head, letting himself be decorated by his grandchildren.

2003, at Frederick Memorial Hospital, his hands still seeming warm, his face at peace as I arrive too late to say goodbye.

# IV

*"…a journey is like marriage.
The certain way to be wrong
is to think you can control it."*

John Steinbeck

# First Night at The Irotama

*(Santa Marta, Colombia, 1979)*

*Perdóname, perdóname,* I begged
for pardon from the thirty collapsing couples
swaying all around us as we tried to reach
the hotel welcome desk.

In the jungle that August night,
a cabbie had dropped us at The Irotama,
a resort lit with Christmas lights,
twenty yards from the beach.

We walked through a hail of salsa music
across the entrance terrace where a dance
marathon was in progress, men and women soaked
in sweat with numbers on their backs.

*You have no reservations,* the lady in reception
called above the din as Jane wilted by my side
and I tried to sort the matter out
in halting Spanish.

In time, we found our way in darkness
to our "deluxe" room with two twin beds,
a candle, so romantic, and the bug spray,
Mata Todo. Kills All, I understood.

*We have no air conditioning or lights,*
I spoke, again in halting Spanish,
on the phone at 3 a.m.
to that lady at the desk.

Our room, where we'd pushed our beds together
to make do, had been transformed into a steambath
where we tried to make some sense
of stifling heat and blackness,

a puddle on the floor around the fridge,
and a voice informing me that every night
in Santa Marta there would be no power
from midnight until dawn.

Hanging up, I lit our candle and shared
the news with Jane. She sat up in her bed.
I think she had some reservations.
*Perdóname*, I said.

# In Santa Marta, Gambling

*(Colombia, 1979)*

"Don't speak," the man behind the wheel told me, sizing up the situation. I sat silent as he exited the car, talking in Spanish to the men surrounding us with automatic weapons.

I'd met this driver at the bar at The Irotama where Jane and I were having a drink at sunset. I'm blocking out his name. He said he knew Santa Marta well and that he was an American doing research on the coast. With short brown hair and glasses, dressed in a guayabera and Levis, he looked the part.

"Is there a place where my wife and I could go to the movies?" I asked him, figuring that Jane would get a kick out of seeing an American film with subtitles.

"The cinema was blown up last week," he replied without flinching, "but the casino is open if you want to go to town." Jane declined quickly, saying she wanted to stay behind and relax. Five minutes later, I was pushing the guy's old Toyota as he popped the clutch and we took off in a cloud of exhaust. "That only happens once in a while," he assured me.

The casino was like those on the back roads of Nevada. With polished chrome and mahogany, it consisted of one large room. Decked out in tuxedoes, the dealers stood, waiting to work, trying not to stare at us. We were the only customers in the place.

After a few beers and hands of blackjack, the emptiness was closing in. "I'm ready to go," I said, using Jane as an excuse to head for home. "No problem," the driver replied.

The road to The Irotama was darker than I remembered, and about halfway there, in the pitch black, the headlights caught a full-size tree being lowered by a rope across the road. There was shouting in Spanish, then ten men with machine guns stepped out from the jungle. I had no idea what was being said. All I know is that after talking with my driver, the guys with guns took one last look at me through the passenger-side window, the tree was raised, and we were allowed to pass.

I don't remember talking on the way back to the hotel, and I never saw the driver again. When I got back to the room, Jane was in bed, reading. "How was it?" she asked. I wasn't sure where to begin.

# Spring Rafting on the New

*(New River, WV, May 1980)*

I guessed we were in trouble when
the river guide moaned, *Oh shit*,
and we spun in slow motion,
the raft gliding over backwards
into Greyhound Station,
a four-foot drop into
a whirlpool so strong
it could suck a bus down
and not let go till summer.

Perched in the stern, I paddled
air for that split second of
dropping into the roar
as the raft stood straight up,
the seven in the front screaming
and grabbing for rope,
the guide seeing her New job
flash before her eyes,
Jane and I getting pummeled
beneath the surface, hoping
we might somehow
breathe again.

# Still Life in a Hurricane

*(Lewes, DE, August 1985)*

Dan wasn't going anywhere.
White-haired and in his seventies,
he just sat on the porch
and watched the front roll in.
Having lost his wife to cancer
and finished his military
and medical careers,
having trekked with Admiral Byrd
to Antarctica,
he had seen enough of life
to stay calm and quiet.
He planned to ride this out.

That night when the storm hit,
he sat in the living room
in the near dark, the only light
the glow of the radio dial
as he listened
to calls to evacuate.
I lay awake in the back room
where Jane and the children
were sleeping, the wind howling,
rain lashing against the house,
the sky rumbling,
flashing white.

When the roof started leaking hard enough
to send me looking for buckets,
Jane woke up,
and we considered what to do.
At dawn, the breakers were taking away
two or three feet of the lawn at a time
with forty feet left,
and I told Dan we were leaving.
Jane got the kids ready,

and I packed our station wagon,
now covered with pine needles,
branches, and sand.

Back in our room, I took
what I thought would be
our last photo on this vacation—
wave crests glowing white
against swells of gunmetal ocean,
a window frame of peeling teak,
cracked glass flecked with rain and sea,
an emerald wine bottle,
uncorked and empty,
wax drizzled down its sides,
and through the window, tan and green,
dunes rapidly disappearing.

*Give it a few more minutes*, Dan told us
as we gathered to say goodbye.
And then, like that, the sun broke through,
the sky cleared,
and the surf calmed down.
When we went outside to check the damage,
all signs of the storm were gone
except a four-foot cliff onto the beach
fifteen feet from the house
and that photo in my camera,
an image I call, in honor of Dan,
Still Life in a Hurricane.

# The Woman with Needs

*(Binghamton, NY, 2001)*

Walking into the hotel, I heard a woman's voice and looked up at the second floor to see her in a window. She was thin, probably in her 20s, with long dark hair nearly to her waist. She'd pushed the drapes aside and was attempting to pry the screen open, screaming, not fearfully, but in anger at someone in the room. I imagined it was a man.

Inside the lobby as I checked in, three children were wandering around—a girl maybe 10, a boy 7 or 8, and another girl, about 3. They walked aimlessly, stopping at times to stare into a candy machine or to pick up magazines. It was nearly midnight.

Sure enough, I was assigned a room on the second floor next to the screaming woman. I still could hear her as I struggled with the key.

"Do I have to say it loud enough for everyone to hear?" she shrieked. "I am a woman with needs. It's been 7 days since you even held me. I want to go out to the car with you. We've got to be alone." In answer, a man mumbled, trying to quiet her.

And then the three children were walking down the hall towards me, looking for their room. Of course, it was the woman's.

Quietly, the girls knocked, the screaming stopped, and someone let them in. The son didn't follow. He stood, his forehead against the wall, some three feet away from the door. Moments later, his older sister came to get him. "It's OK, it's OK," she said. "You can come in; they're going out to the car together." She put her arm around him and took him in.

In my room, as I got ready for bed, I heard the next room's hall door open and shut.

With their parents gone, the room got loud again, the three kids giggling, jumping from bed to bed. Things finally settled at 1 a.m., and at 3, the door slammed as the parents returned. This time the father's voice was hard, the

48

mother's more subdued.

In the morning, I got up early and left, passing by the family's room, now silent. To this day, I try not to hear that lady's voice or see her in that window. But I'm haunted by her little boy, who turned to a wall for comfort.

# Outside the Visitor Center

*(Grand Canyon, March 16, 2016)*

Like all of us,
this man had come to the Canyon
to be amazed.

Outside the Visitor Center,
I heard the cries for help
and saw the gathering crowd.

Inside, I got a ranger
who grabbed the defibrillator
and commanded, *Show me where.*

By now the man lay lifeless
on the cement by a water fountain,
his shirt off, his friends stunned,

a stranger doing CPR,
the ranger getting the paddles
ready:

*Stand clear.*
Shock.
Nothing.

Like all of us,
this man had come to the Canyon
to be amazed.

*Stand clear.*
Shock.
Nothing.

# Found Poem:
# Signs on the Pacific Coast Scenic Byway

*(Rte. 101, OR, July 19-20, 2017)*

Rocks
Elk
Beaver

Devil's Punchbowl
Tillamook Cheese
Smelt Sands

Flounder Inn
Tsunami Hazard Zone
Gopher Problem?

Cannabis Dispensary
Five Dollars a Joint
Firearms and Groceries


Roads End

# V

*"In dreams we are true poets..."*

Ralph Waldo Emerson

# Dream Poem: The Dancing Trees

*(1992)*

The trees are dying and I
know it. First, the pink dogwood
by the steps comes down,
limb after limb gone to anthracnose,
bark girdled, then peeling off.
From her stump, shoots sprout for years,
drawing strength from what rots
beneath the ground.

Spraying can't save
the purple plum.
The bores have got her.
Each September
through the frost,
she bleeds and drools,
her amber sap
catching western light.

The red oak dies for decades.
Towering over the house,
she gives up one side at a time.
First the northwest branches go,
the two huge ones over the bedroom,
lush leaves still springing
from the upper limbs.
*Trim and feed her*, the tree men say.

At night, in dreams,
the trees are dancing,
swirling, fainting
in pirouettes.
In the center,
I'm standing, rooted,
unable to save them
as they're drawn into the Earth.

# Dream Poem: The Jones Falls

*(1992)*

It's 3 a.m. and I'm doing 85
on the JFX, roaring down
the concrete funnel into Baltimore.
Green road signs flick by
like movies in the halogen glow.
As the buildings loom,
the traffic thickens,
rows of cars and eighteen-wheelers
racing bumper to bumper,
hell-bent for the harbor.
Rounding the curve before
the prison, I'm closing ground
on the moving column
when my eyes slam shut
and I cannot make them open.
*Wake up!* I'm screaming to
myself, prying at my eyes
with thumbs and fingers.
*Wake up!*

Just ahead
taillights
begin to flare.

# Dream Poem: Going Off the Meds

*(1999)*

In this dream, I risk my life
to take control of a snarling,
spitting mountain lion
that has leapt onto the back
of a weak old horse
and is savaging it,
clawing, biting,
bringing it to its knees.

Somehow I manage to leash
the cat, pulling it from the horse
and straining to hold it
at arm's length from myself
as it rages,
wanting to destroy me.
If I keep it nearly strangled,
I'll be safe.

# Dream Poem: Picture Day

*(2005)*

Something is not right this picture day.
On the hill, outside the school entrance,
the administrators are posing
for portraits, tied onto the backs of yaks
in the thundering, driving rain.
*Action photos*, the feature editor demands,
so the yaks are prodded
until they stampede and slide,
legs splayed, while the principal
and vice principals do their best
to appear in total, oblivious control.
*I didn't get the shot!*
the photo dunce cries out.
*Take two!* shouts Madam Editor,
and the staff begins pushing
the now resistant beasts once more
to the top of the hill.


Meanwhile under the portico
beneath the school sign
with its cast aluminum letters,
it's time for department pictures,
mathematics to be exact,
and all goes well until two
algebra guys, nearing sixty
and fifty pounds overweight,
come out of the school, dressed
just in black thongs
and take their places before the camera,
turning their backs and bending over.


*Attention, all students, attention:*
the P.A. system blares,
*This year we're taking our candid
shots at the circus. Anyone who wants to go,*

*please board the buses immediately!*
Out of nowhere thirty buses appear,
and fourteen hundred students rush madly
to climb on board.

On the fourth floor, in his lonely tower,
the yearbook advisor considers his fate
and signs his resignation.

# Dream Poem: Waves on the Thirtieth Floor

*(2017)*

Jane and I are making love
in a king-size bed
in a luxury room
on the thirtieth floor
of a high-rise hotel,
probably in Manhattan.
All the walls are windows,
and we've neglected
to close the curtains.

In a brief pause,
I look to the right
and realize that
we're directly across the street
from a glass-walled restaurant
where two men have stopped
their meal to watch us.
Those men seem fully
entertained.

Shocked, I grab Jane's elbow
and pull her off the bed
to try to hide.
*People are watching us*, I tell her.
*No they aren't*, Jane replies,
claiming they can't see us.
*They can*, I insist, and to prove it,
I encourage her to look
across the street with me.

So, like two prairie dogs,
we pop our heads up
over the bed to take a look.
By now, the restaurant's windows
are packed with people.

*They can't see this far*, Jane persists.
*Wave to them*, I say to prove my point,
so we both wave and, of course,
the whole crowd in the restaurant
waves back.

# VI

*"Laughter is the sun
that drives winter
from the human race."*

Victor Hugo

# Advice and Guarantee Wastecan

Don't go swimming on a full stomach.
Don't drink on an empty stomach.
Eat carrots; they're good for your eyes.
Drink this; it'll put hair on your chest.
Don't talk back to your mother.
Never tell a lie.
This won't hurt a bit.
Keep both hands on the wheel.
Plan ahead.
Don't worry.
Always keep 'em guessing.
Stay away from older women.
Don't take yourself so seriously.
Wipe that smile off your face.
Never write poems that are simply lists.

# He Sensed He Was in Trouble

He sensed he was in trouble
when all his emails went unanswered,
even ones to brothers and sisters,
and all his phone calls led to
*Please leave a message.*
No one got back to him
*as soon as possible*
though he kept his landline passable
and his cell phone charged.
Neighbors turned their lights out
when he approached, their dogs
snarling for no apparent reason.
His trickle of mail dried up
unless you count repeated requests
from Globe Life and Accident Insurance
for him to take out a policy
on his nonexistent children,
five or ten thousand dollars each.
When he asked for extra cheese,
the pizza delivery place hung up.
*Not again!* the 9-1-1 operator spit out
when his Weber grill caught fire.
The National Do Not Call Registry
refused to reverse his decision.
Most days he sat with his K-Mart
letter opener and two phones
at his keyboard, waiting
to pounce on anything incoming.
At night he slept with his rosary,
which seemed to be losing beads.

# Dear Mail Lady

*(Towson, MD, 2015)*

You might want to be careful
when you deliver our mail today.
For the last two years, a toad the size of a plum
has made a home in our mailbox,
sitting still through your daily torrent
of magazines, bills, and letters.

Today our toad is gone,
and in his place is a two-foot snake,
looking fat and satisfied.
I'm fairly certain that he is harmless,
most likely a DeKay's brown snake,
according to a herpetologist at the Baltimore Zoo.

My neighbor tells me she's not so sure,
that according to the Internet,
pythons have been proliferating in the wild.
Nonsense, I say, that's in the Everglades.
And anyway, the last time I opened the mailbox,
I distinctly heard a rattle.

# The Perfect American Poem

The American woman is perfect.
She is a CEO, an interior designer,
a gourmet cook and fashion model,
a child behavior specialist.
Capable of performing
forty tasks at once,
she sleeps soundly in her king-size bed.

The American man is perfect.
Tall and tautly muscled,
he is a skilled carpenter and lover,
a fierce athlete and plumber.
Never deigning to shed a tear,
he cruises, in control,
astride his riding mower.

American children are perfect.
With pretty teeth and test scores,
they are all-star shortstops, presidents
of honor societies, and certainly Ivy-bound.
Having mastered the art of pleas
and thank-yous, they sit thoughtfully,
reading the family Bible.

The American poem is perfect.
It is serious and steeped in meaning,
pruned to polite perfection.
Wrought with reason
with a touch of rhyme to season,
like the people it considers,
it is perfect in every conceivable way.

# The Man Who Couldn't Stop Revising

The Man Who Couldn't Stop Revising
Who Couldn't Stop Revising
The Man Who Couldn't Stop
The Man Who Couldn't
The Man Couldn't
The Man
Stop the Man
The Man, Revising
The Revising Man
Revising, Stop the Man
Stop Revising
Revising, Stop
Stop Who
Stop the Man
Who Couldn't
Stop

# VII

*"Have patience with everything
that remains unsolved in your heart."*

Rainer Maria Rilke

# Age 65, With Both Parents Gone

What once was an ocean,
its far shore only imagined,
is now a stream.

What once was a night sky
filled with distant stars
is now a door.

# How I Hope It Will Be

Drifting to the ground
like an oak leaf in November,
deep in the hills
beyond all trails,
in time disappearing
into Earth.

# A Promise to My Grandchildren

I will not let
an old man's shadow
deny the light to February's flowers.

Let's go outside
to look for snowdrops.
Aren't those robins in the trees?

# Reading the Paper, 66

I turn first to sports,
then skim the editorials
and scan the news—

murders, car bombs,
revolutions,
natural disasters.

Next, I check the obit page
with its photos and titles
in forty-eight font,

names followed by quick summaries
of what each family wants
remembered.

That done, I head outside to find
the sky fierce blue, a red-shouldered hawk
calling in the distance.

# Like Thomas, Reading Signs

*(Bristol, TN, March 2015)*

Raised up in gold and incense,
I've been offered the wine of afterlife,
the victory of Easter, the promises
of a Second Coming.

Not taking much on faith,
I often hope that death will be
a simple flipping of a switch–
the end.

This cloudy Lenten morning
on Interstate 81,
a billboard proclaimed with certainty,
*When you die, you will meet God.*

A few miles north on a fenced-in hilltop,
a Confederate flag proclaimed
that the South, too,
will rise again.

# Two Rosaries

*(in honor of Deifilia Zevallos de Coronel,1856-1952)*

For years my prayers
were brief and broken
as I struggled to stay on track
sending thoughts into the night.
And then my mother,
in her eighties,
gave me a set of glass black beads,
the rosary her mother, Anastasia,
prayed at Mass and each afternoon
in her rocking chair.

And when my mother passed away,
she left me a rosary of mother-of-pearl
in a small worn envelope.
It had been left to her by Anastasia,
a gift from my Great-Grandmother Deifilia,
and labeled in my grandmother's
unmistakable script
as a rosary from *Mamita*,
her mother-in-law in Ecuador,
who was as precious to her as a mother.

Now often before I sleep
or before dawn when I lie awake,
I pray with one of those rosaries,
traveling through the decades
connected with others
who have prayed this way through history
and especially with two women
whose lives spanned centuries
and for whom faith was as important and natural
as breathing.

# Something Almost Spiritual

There's something almost spiritual
in our bodies barely touching
in the first moments of quiet
after making love.

There's something almost spiritual
in our children's peaceful breathing,
their faces bathed in the glow of sleep
as we cover them for the night.

There's something almost spiritual
at the finish of a poem
as thoughts settle like falling leaves
in the sudden silence.

# Acknowledgments

Special thanks to:

Noah Belt, a fine photographer, teacher, and friend, and Mary Lou Coyle, a restoration wizard at Coyle Studios, for turning a photo I shot in 1985 into my cover photo.

Gary Blankenburg, who has mentored me in writing for over 30 years, and whose brotherhood, skill, and gentle wisdom helped shape my manuscript.

Sara Jones Cleary, my daughter, a keen-eyed and supportive editor, who shared her expertise and love as this book came into being.

Thanks also to the editors of the following publications in which the listed pieces first appeared, some in slightly different form:

*Abbey:* "The Benefit," "Don't Consider This"

*Baseball Bard:* "Playing Right"

*Borderlands: Texas Poetry Review:* "The Perfect American Poem"

*Caesura:* "Like Thomas, Reading Signs"

*Chiron Review:* "Thought, Skydiving"

*The Comstock Review:* "He Sensed He Was in Trouble"

*The Kerf:* "Manta Ray"

*Lilliput Review:* "How I Hope It Will Be"

*Loch Raven Review:* "Age 65, With Both Parents Gone," "Why William Wordsworth Never Lived in Baltimore"

*Passager:* "The Woman with Needs"

*Slant: A Journal of Poetry:* "Dream Poem: The Dancing Trees"

*Studio One:* "My Last Visit with My Grandfather Jones"

*Swimming at Night* (chapbook, winner of a Baltimore Artscape Literary Arts Award for Poetry): "Advice and Guarantee Wastecan," "Car Crash, Christmas Eve"

*Word Up Baltimore: A Poetry Collection:* "Dream Poem: The Jones Falls"

# About the Author

Bill Jones has been the author of two collections of poetry—*Swimming at Night*, a chapbook that won a Baltimore Artscape Literary Arts Award for Poetry, and *At Sunset, Facing East*, a memoir in poetry published by Apprentice House Press in 2016. Over the past thirty years, his writing has appeared in numerous small press magazines and journals across the country. He lives in Baltimore with his wife, Jane Croghan Jones.

![Apprentice House Press logo]

Apprentice
House Press
*Loyola University Maryland*

Apprentice House is the country's only campus-based, student-staffed book publishing company. Directed by professors and industry professionals, it is a nonprofit activity of the Communication Department at Loyola University Maryland.

Using state-of-the-art technology and an experiential learning model of education, Apprentice House publishes books in untraditional ways. This dual responsibility as publishers and educators creates an unprecedented collaborative environment among faculty and students, while teaching tomorrow's editors, designers, and marketers.

Outside of class, progress on book projects is carried forth by the AH Book Publishing Club, a co-curricular campus organization supported by Loyola University Maryland's Office of Student Activities.

Eclectic and provocative, Apprentice House titles intend to entertain as well as spark dialogue on a variety of topics. Financial contributions to sustain the press's work are welcomed. Contributions are tax deductible to the fullest extent allowed by the IRS.

To learn more about Apprentice House books or to obtain submission guidelines, please visit www.apprenticehouse.com.

Apprentice House
Communication Department
Loyola University Maryland
4501 N. Charles Street
Baltimore, MD 21210
Ph: 410-617-5265 • Fax: 410-617-2198
info@apprenticehouse.com•www.apprenticehouse.com